Changes

By: Tasha C. Mapes

Published by Dragon Soul Publishing

Changes
Copyright 2014 Tasha Mapes
ISBN 978-0-9955500-0-1
Published 1st September 2016
Dragon Soul Publishing

Publisher's address:
11 Nichol Place
Cotford St Luke
Taunton
Somerset
TA4 1JD

Moon Sonnet

Silvery light strikes a chord
In moment's hidden away
A wolf's call to a moon adored
Fading before the new day.
The sun sings songs that never touch
The darkened depths of night
The moon holds sway over the stars and such
Shedding its own cold light.
Muted tones of the sun's goodbye
As the brightest colors run
The night hiding more truths and a lie
Than the starkness of the sun.
And the deepest moments of our dreams
Are made of the same stuff as moonbeams.

Night Moments

As the candles go out
One by one
Now is the dusk
Gone is the sun
In the quiet moments
The monsters hide
Waiting for the moon
To turn a bloodier tide.
Ashes to ashes
All is dust
Sinews and nerves
Knotted by lust
In the darker moments
The monsters take flight

2 Gorging on freedom

Until chained by the Light.

Endangered

In the eyes the window to the soul,
Blackened and hidden by a shadow of kohl,
Deep in the dark where secrets are kept
Down in the well where the hidden tiger leapt
Hidden from all who walk under the sun
Shying away and known by none
Shallow the light much the dark
Up through the Earth towards the silent mark
Flying through heavens shaded by night
Crawling through forests spiraled by light
Wounded by time and dying away
Never here forever and never to stay
Running through fields flowers of gold
Swimming through rivers location never told
Unable to speak unable to fight
Unable to say what they need is right
Shackled and caged by another's fate
Action undertaken might be too late

Inside

Last summer sunshine
Stretches, drifts
Past my window
Never quite reaching inside
While I stare
Soaking in the sight
If not the feel
Imagining I was out there
Free and warmed
Instead of here.

Misery

Misery
My heart's new companion
Tears shreds out of me
Bad memories of old
Pale before a new kind of
Damage
One not faced before
That stretches
What I hold
What I can bear
So determined it won't break me
But still I crack
Little pieces that
Play their part
To make me less
Than I was
And that I thought I was

4 Constant
In lines that slowly fade
My control
Slipping when I take a new
Fall
A free fall
Like the tears I have no room left
To hold.

Healing

Colors surround
Every part of me
As I fall
Weightless and uncaring
Not into darkness
But colors more pure
More real
Than what my eyes
Have always seen
Letting go and laying back
As my free fall
Lifts me
And sets me free
Leaving me not less
But more complete
Than before
As the color's vibrancy
Sinks into
Every crack of my soul.

Transient

Silent hearts
That are
Filled
With everything-
Endless questions
And Hopeful answers
Pain and memories of it
Slowly bow before
Creeping peace
And flashes of joy.

Too Afraid to Fly (The World)

Too afraid to fly
So we lie
Say we don't know how to dance
So we never take the chance
Hiding behind masks
Unwilling to face our own difficult tasks
We ignore any hope we've found
We help ourselves to be bound
Allow no one to see your face
Don't give knowledge of emotion, in any case
Lies of the world we're told
Ignoring the lives we've sold
To get here
To protect our own fear
Too afraid to fly-
So we lay down and die.

6 Grace

Through this land
Both tried and tempered
Held the hand that kept a hold on
Sheltered by the simplest grace
That under sky
No fears could cling to
Hastened forward
Cold the fury
Found no grip to pull it steady
Shook the earth
And fled impotent
Sheltered by this purest grace
That led on through
Hottest trials
Making paths through
Angel's stations
Took the chance for highest glory
Saw the moment and realized beauty
Through all terrors pulled me safely
Held my hand when I couldn't hold on
Pulled me through the low and dark land
Sheltered by the loveliest grace
To the highland lit by lovelight
Into Grace's embrace.

Dim Moonlight

Dim moonlight
Glancing off snowy
Fields,
A different kind of dark
That rests in the silence
Of a wonderland,
Even the night asleep
Save one lone squirrel
Hopping and leaping
Through snow drifts
Bathed in the
Dim moonlight.

Grief

You were gone and I waited
I waited for the Sun
To stop it's silly shining
For the Moon to give up all it's pining
And fall from the sky
I waited for the stars
To blink out one by one
And follow into darkness
The once majestic Sun
I waited for the waves
To stop their crashing
To support by silence
My soul's smashing
Grief.

8 The Enemies

They stand apart
Facing each other
Enemies who share the same home
Over the mile wide
5 foot gulf
Between them
They fling daggers
At each other
Cutting and being cut
Just to see the other
Bleed
The world does not end
It explodes
Each volatile missile
Hitting it's mark
And opening a new gash
As I stand a
Silent witness
To the malicious
Destruction.
After minutes and hours
The last of the
Explosions tearing
Final chunks
From my world,
The enemies
Go to bed together
To lick the wounds
They have created.

The Field

A field that is
Lays peaceful
Long grasses grow
Yellow-colored in the Fall
And I am falling too
Into a quiet that
Pervades my chittering soul
Hard concrete
And cold buildings
Burn my imaginings
With pictures of blank
Faces, unreal and
Staring right through
I hear a bird
It sounds like the
Calling of my own name
Somehow I am sure
These creatures
Know me
Recognize some simpler
Part of my Being
That joy I feel
In Nature's presence
Is the coming home
All humanities world
A cold hotel
Where you are not known
Nay, nor cared for in
Any particular way
This field, or any
Is a return, a Restoration

10 Coming to peace of all
My failings and complexities
I long to return
To the Home-Field
Of my childish
Rememberings-
Yet there is nothing
Where the Birds and
Beasts knew me
Where a seldom tree
Sheltered and
Nature whispered again
Of my truest origins-
Now there is nothing.
Only the cold of a
Man-made world.
The Beasts have been turned
Out, the Birds have flown
There is no peace
In our busy
Conquerings
And I cannot hear the call
Her call
And my tranquil connections
Through the feet deep
Unfeeling
Concrete.

Dusty ages
Spent by rages
Wracking the dusty air
Time passing by
Filled with a silent lie
Stripping all that's ugly bare
Leaving only truth-
That's hidden in youth.

No Need of Truth in Youth

Tell me why should youth
Have any need or hold on truth
For all that truth implies
Are a thousand broken ties
Of what should be and discipline
O, not for the young that sin!
No, I would say rather let
Ignorance keep the youth from all that may fret;
For what good can come of
A child denied childhood's love
With age all ugly becomes bare
Showing only full honesty what's there
Nay, nay! Not for the youth
Is the insipid empty truth!

12 Getting Back

Hollowed, cracked and faded
Pieces of me
Fall apart without You
A graying memory
Of the way things were
Me in my old room
Kneeling
I'd never been more strong
I walk alone today
You always near,
It's me far away
Not sure when it started
Or when I failed to search
Your presence in my life
The only good thing
Pure thing left
As my presence in this world grows
Cracked and dirty
I start to look around
Surprised and lonely
I've wandered this far.
A step back to You
But it feels like miles
And I'll get there if I crawl
Back on my knees
Dragging all the
Pieces of me.

Eighteen, nineteen, blue sky
Pieces shake and shatter
Arrows in the night
Bright
Light
Pool together in mystifying cumulative degrees
Of verbally degrading arsenal
Breaking the insipid and dull
Keep on and let it roll
Pay the toll
Lose your soul
Find the diamond in the coal
Smooth apart
The wrinkles in the heart
And it'll change
The veins
That carry blood
It is a flood
Turns my world to mud
Thirteen, fourteen, dark sky
Deny it's mine
Everything's fine
Keep to the line
No stars
In my way are bars
Sixteen, fix me, twilight sky
Falling stars at night
Light
Bright
So, so, bright.

14 Sculptor's Work

Graceful lines
Unmoving features
Shaped with care,
A tender artist's hands
Moving the form
Towards creation
A figure of marble
Expression all empathetic grace
Empty
But filled with
A creator's visions
An exquisite sculpture
To be stared at.
For some lifeless,
For some an embodiment
Of the sculptor's ambition,
Or still
The sculptor's love.

Winter Expanse

Frozen winter expanse
An endlessly stretching
Blanket, unbroken-
The most pure thing
Only pure thing
An alien landscape
Undiminished as of yet
By the creeping stain
Of travelers boot prints
And graying sludge kicked
Into existence
Over the startling beauty.

Euphoric

Euphoric crescents of crimson
Bloom across my chest
Shades of pain in liquid form
Take from me my best
Stunning moment, fall from grace
Fill my failing lungs
Nothing more that you can take
Silence all the tongues
I feel no fear at close of day
Though you shudder hard
Your regret far outweighs mine
Your soul, not mine, marred.
I see in many colours now
Where there were such grays
My tears are reddened like my cuts

16 Still I sing His praise.

Cinderella

Burn light too bright
Sunshine breaks time
My heart far apart
One chance we dance
Moon falls love calls
Starry sky I cry
Midnight tolls.

Evil Stepmother

Mirror mirror on the wall
No one hears me when I call
I have wandered all alone
For my crimes I must atone
I have tried to change my ways
Tried to learn hatred never pays
But I have darkness in my heart
Of which I do not know the start
These things that drive me as they do
And led to my ill treatment of you
Happy endings will ever pass me by
The role I play my curse 'til I die.

Antiquated
I am old
I am relic
Throwback to
Different thoughts.
I hold on
To morals
Rejected
And politenesses
Now unnecessary.
I relish
That which has
Stood time's test
Mourning
The new and blank.

18 Night Blizzard

Deep black
Blinding
White flakes
Driven by icy wind
As though shot
From out of
The darkest pit
Swirling all around
A winter night
Of ice
Stabbing cold
And snowy particles
Whipping past
And whirling back around
At the whim
Of a capricious wind
The core "me"
At the center
As it passes by and around
Like stars flying though a
Universe of obsidian
Though cold,
There is peace in the
Snowy dark, tonight.

Everyone roots for an underdog.
No one roots for the easy jog.
It is the struggle, the tough slog
That makes us root for an underdog.

Everyone roots for the least well off
The one that the bettors mock and scoff
The one with willpower and a cough
We will root for the one who's least well off.

Everyone roots for the hard of luck
We see ourselves when they're said to suck
We love them for their hopeful pluck
Let's root for the ones who are hard of luck.

Everyone roots for an underdog
Who makes it through every obstacle and bog
Who stumbles on through every fog
We will always root for the underdog.

20 Shut Off

The day darkens
Coming to a close
Your eyes shut off
Hiding all your foes.
You can not cope
With these failures yet
Your ears shut off
You say you're all set
For your rising
But you're set to fall
Your mind shuts off
You ignore my call.

I Want to Leave Them Singing

I want to burn out like a light
Quickly but blazing bright
Like a candle in the darkest night
I want to laugh at
Slow sweet Eternity
That evades us all for the
Duration of our journey
And boldly state it
Was never what I wanted anyway
I want to scream at the Moon
But deny any proffered boon
I want to be one they say went too soon
I want to leave when my blood is still tingling
When fire and fight in my veins are zinging
I want to leave them singing.

You are dawn and I am dust
The new and the bright
I am rust
You are morning, noon and sun
I am the ending, I am dusk
You are the whole,
Uncracked, unvarnished
I am splintered as
Yesterday's lust
I am fallen
Saint now sinner
You the praised and I the cussed
Your bonds have dropped
They wind me tighter
Round the centre
Sinking low my glory taken
You shine brighter
My heart stopped
Rising higher full moon sky
I the dark, planet imploding
You are now, tomorrow's topped
I the yesteryear
Discovered lie
You the opening of life
I am the settling dust
You the star, arise to light
I am rust, an ending plight.

22 New Dawn Breaking

New dawn breaking
Hope in the rays that filter down
As I find myself waking
Strangely, as though
I'd been sleeping
For ages, too long
And now back to consciousness
I'm creeping
My eyes opening with a
Remembered ache
Cautiously, waiting for the pain
Or to lose
Something for someone else's sake.
But the day is bright
And no immediate pain is coming
And the sky out the window
Is a beautiful sight
Clear, clear, such an odd feeling
To slowly come awake
The end of the foggy
Existence with which I'd been dealing
I close my eyes and take a breath,
This new chance is the best of life
But there's a moment in it
That's a little of death.

Devotion

Devotion is seventeen years.
It is a garden grown
Time after time
Careful construction and
Observation
From seed to flower to fruit.
Devotion is the watchful eye
And the hand that makes notes.
It is patience
That lasts life spans.
Green and yellow
Smooth and wrinkled.
Devotion is the austere life
The contemplation,
The dedication that does not fade
Without accolades
Taking us down to our roots,
To the alleles in us.
It is my mother
It is my father
I am genotype Tt.
Is devotion dominant?
Is it hidden, recessive?
Devotion is a name for Mendel.
No sign of it in his phenotype.
Devotion can change our world.

24 Our coding does not match up

We cannot bind together.
The codons unzipped in me
Proclaim AUC
They filter through the
Nuclei scattered in my being.
I search for my anticodons
But the tRNA can not bring
You to me.
You are free floating,
Unmatching,
AGC.
We cannot bind together.
Our coding does not match up.

Mocking Bird

Mocking bird you have it best
Lording it over all the rest
Mocking bird your laugh so cruel
Coming with a gun to a sword fight duel
Mocking bird watch your own
The people come looking for you to stone.

Printed posies on her pocket

Little girl skips in time
The wind is still
The flowers sing
She makes a little rhyme.
Blue sky, new sky,
Today, tomorrow, and on
Blue sky, new sky,
After the flowers all have gone
Dark sky, night sky,
Until the stars are done
Dark sky, night sky,
Until there's only one.
Printed posies on her pocket,
Little girl goes home
The wind is high
The flowers dance
Their petals start to roam.

Two Parts

Bars of steel or bars of gold
Makes no difference but that I was sold
The bird grabbed for its song on the wing
Once caged would not sing.

Hot summer skies or Autumn just as fair
Spring in its budding or winter so bare
Captured, I would not love betray
But once freed it would not stay.

26 Angel Mine

Angel Mine I loved you before the world began
Before your shape had taken form I held you in my hand
I listened to your hopes and dreams before you met the world
You are the loveliest of My roses that ever did unfurl.
Child Mine I knew you before light had touched the land
A single shining seed among millions of grains of sand
I watched you take your first steps on bold and shaky feet
Remembering how I cradled you near, where light and
darkness meet.
Beloved One I've heard your cries, scattered over time
Did you think I wasn't there, blessed little star of Mine?
You've scraped your knees and scraped your heart, you've
laughed and you have cried
But beyond your soul's understanding is My love and, too, My
pride.

Tightly

Metal chains
Around a heart
Are wrapped
Tightly.

Loss

The shards
Of shattered disillusionment
Cut deep
Blood running
Like crimson tears
From your broken soul
Endless pieces
Scattered to the
Four corners of an empty world
A pointless search
For hope in the dying light
A devastated moment
Illuminates tainted dreams
Poison spreading from the entry wound
Through the veins
Like stifled breath
The fading of a last chance
Lost to eternity.

28 Endless Endless Fears

What am I so afraid of
The future on the wings of a dove
Comes swooping in
But I can hear nothing above the din
Of the voices murmuring in my ears
Endless, endless are my fears.

In my sight a million roads
But all surrounded by inflexible codes
While I am stuck on just this one
Uncertain of which way to run
Blinded by wearisome tears
Endless, endless are my fears.

Reaching out for something I can't see
Looking for what and where I'm supposed to be
Every different opinion that portrays
Me, in a million different ways
Indecisiveness' ugly head rears
Endless, endless are my fears.

So many choices I can't make
Too many paths I'm too afraid to take
But I can't stand forever in one place
The future, my future is something I must face
Knowing I must find a way, my soul it sears
To find a way to put to rest
My endless, endless fears.

My Angel

It was winter when I saw her
My angel turned away
The frosty air hung crisp and clear
Angry, I had nothing to say.
She hummed a tune low and sweet
I thought I'd known the words
But my memory couldn't tell me
Only that it was unmatchable by a thousand birds.
I sometimes felt her presence since
Or saw feathers near my eye
But I still had nothing to say
Though I thought I heard her sigh.
She never stayed for long,
The times she came to me
Always my angel was turned away
Never her face did I see.
I practised my words a hundred times
How to explain my fury?
The angel was glory beloved-
I a criminal to my own inner jury.
I stumbled to my knees one day
Driven past my strength
"Heaven helps you always" she whispered
"You're loved beyond ocean's length."
I couldn't reach for the gentle hand
Held out for me to take
Still angry she'd always been turned away
Still hoping it for my sake.
I took her hand
My anger fled
Cared for by her

30 **And** sweetly led.
She brought me to a garden
Where I was fed and healed
Then saw the gates of heaven
The other side of a golden field
I questioned her about it
Not sure if I should go
She promised me if it was time
I wouldn't question but know.
Like a child I held tight to her robe
And whispered to see her face
Her giggle chimed, a bell's sweet chirp
The answer, once home in that place.
I backed away and found in my legs
The strength to carry on
Seeing only glimpses over the years
Til my heart was tired and wan.
When sleep had come to claim me
My angel did return
She held me til my eyes closed
Slipping from concern.
I woke up as she carried me
Beyond the gates of grace
And once there, my soul freed,
I touched gently her loving face.

Church tower bell ring
Echoes through the building
Worn pews lit by
Dancing shadows from
Stained glass windows
Candlesticks partially burned
And dried wax drips
Unnoticed down the
Dark wood alter,
Red carpet roll
More subdued than the
Gaudy Hollywood walk,
Arched doors and heavy handles
The memories of
Multitudes of feet
Passing through
Plain wooden cross
Standing center of attention
Touched by transient
Searching hands like
Butterfly wings brushing over
Leaving faded prayers
Clinging to the beloved cross
Dust mote air
An odd mix of
Contemplation and expectation
While long ago and recent
Hymn chords seem to linger
Not more than a breath
But present, hovering
Quiet and comforting

32 An indefinable quality
The seekers of a peace
That have left a residue
Of themselves
Joyful praise and sorrowful prayer
Mingling, reaching
Carved walls and a tableau of tapestries
Weave a picture
More compelling than
An ordinary artist
Can create
A haven built from themselves
Dreams of untold souls
Who have sheltered there
For their own brief moments in time.

The Birth of the Fairy Queen

It floated down a little bit
Then hovered back and on its way
It seldom stopped to take a sit
This fairy I followed today.

It didn't seem to notice me
The pretty wood-green fairy
And I wouldn't catch something so free
But curious at what it tried to carry.

It dragged in air a small thin twig
(I crept cautiously behind)
And once it stopped to eat a fig
If it noticed me it didn't mind.

At last the tiny wings held their flutter
A bell chime sounded out
And more appeared as I began to mutter
A ceremony, I had no doubt.

My wood-green fairy held high her prize
That silly little twig-
And soon the place filled with joyful cries
And two little fairy men began to dig.

They stuck the twig in the new made hole
Then all danced crazily 'round it
Knew I then the dance in my soul
But now comes the best bit-

The twig burst forth in sudden life

34 And blossoms exploded gaily
Sudden tension in the glade rife
I remember this part daily-

A purple blossom uncurling
All were silent, all were still
Tiny new wings unfurling
Sudden bright rays chasing away any chill

She sat on the edge of her flower
And all bowed for the crown on her head
She stood up new birthed in power
But I never heard what her crystal voice said.

I woke up at the edge of the wood
Memory teasing me on
I took off as fast as I could
Desperate as though to outrun the dawn

Wanting to prove it no dream or riddle
And finally came to a quiet glade
With a blossoming twig in the middle
Where homage to a new queen was paid.

Affordable Desire

I desire a new wardrobe
Full of cool new gear;

I desire something to wear
Anything warm will do, and give a little cheer.

I want an expensive new pet
Maybe a corgi- round like a log

I want something to spend time with
Wish I could afford a friend like a dog.

I'd like to try exotic dishes
And never eat anything but my favourite food

I'd like to have a meal tonight
Anything would brighten my hungry stomach's mood
I wish my room was bigger
There's hardly room for all my stuff!

I wish I had somewhere to live
Life on the streets can be so rough.

I desire, desire, desire
There's so much that I still want

I need, need, need
For me life's not a pleasant easy jaunt.

36 Angel Sight

An angel wept over me
For all the things I could not be
I didn't understand his tears
I've never felt all his fears
I am human; body and soul
For what sins of mine will that eternal bell toll
I've made my choices and what are they
That I should be ashamed by light of day
I've gone my way, stumbled and fell
I know others who've done worse as well
But I alone will pay for my slippery path
Only One knows if I'm fruit or chaff
But I am certain of one thing
If future and history make a ring
I would forever choose the same
Give up all, my heart, my true name,
For you, commit the truest human crime
And pay back in eternity all my sin's time.

Chaos in the mind
Unwinds and flows
Through rivers in the brain
The insane that order
Their minds
To fit in little boxes
That are packed
For the move to
Another place
Prettier or the same
A tame panther
In a kitty carrier
That runs wild when
No one's looking
Dashes by a lake
That wasn't there before
Like the memories
You don't have
Turn to dust in forgotten boxes
That haven't been moved
Since I remember
The panther fed on
Rabbit food
Stalking a purple flower
Knocks a box that was left
There and
Hasn't been unpacked since
The day
You first saw the river
That wasn't there
The panther sitting lamely

38 Beside

That races the moon
That isn't seen
Its eye measuring
The ordered things
That aren't remembered
A feeling of moonlight
Is a light flower's brush
Turned hard by sunlight
A flower that was
Carved by an artist
That only ever touched stone
Felt the same
As the boxes that were
Never packed
While at the zoo the
Panther runs wild
Showing its tame face
To daylight and clouds
For sanity's peace of mind
Which is non-existent
Only the crazy find
Acceptance of the lonely peace
That fills the
Like the crowds in their minds
Are yours
Like a panther
You once knew
That had a different face
Than the one I knew.

Pages in a book
That turn
A wind...
Blows them open...
And you are there.
Beautiful light
Falls on empty words
That I read once...
But I never understood
What you were always saying...
A desk of wood-green
With scattered pages
Laying jumbled on its top
Flipped through by a
Careless hand
I reached for air...
You were not there.
Dancing leaves
Fall through an
Open window
To the desk
Gently stirring the
Yellow faded pages
Unbearable in truthful words
That cracked
My pretty picture...
A lovely picture
I never showed you
What you saw...
My soul in a book...
I was never ready to read...

40 Pages that held
Time's story...
 asked you to read
And you turned pages...
While I turned away...
The desk in front of
A closed window
Cloaked seasons
Only empty pages saw...
An empty room
Filled with things from a time
When you stood there
With me...
I forgot all but
A child's story
That tease them out an
Open window
I look out
And see you
Like before
No memory held such power
In frozen time
You eased the book
To the desk
I was missing so long
I *grabbed*
Solid in my fingers...
Eases raindrops and teardrops
From their holding place...
Blurring words seen on
Empty pages...
Empty without my understanding
I know better now...

And I waited...
For the book's pages to clear
Always I turned
From the window I never
Accepted as closed...
And you were there.

Entanglements

Twisting lines
Creeping and slinking
Into place
Shadowed movements
Knotting around the core
Winding tighter
With imperceptible manoeuvres
Until the cords
Are indistinguishable
From the organic instrument
Beating under the layers
Of imposed entanglements.

42 Those Words

Those words were stones
Dropping hard into the well
Of your soul.
They were mistakes,
But they made ripples.
I could not pull them back
Or settle the water.

No apologies
Could soothe the distorted image
So I would not try
And offend you
With my need for absolution.

Excuses and reasons
Are all the same.
It is about making clear
One's side of things
I do not understand my side either,
So I will let you have yours
Unfettered.

Those words
Fell blunt from my lips
Too honest and confused
But the meaning was clear
And they sank deep.

An empty room
Filled with silence
Returns silent questions
I refused to ask
Silence stops the screams
Of a crowded mind
No one enters
The room sitting
Alone, holding no answers;
Memories of someone there
Pulling at a mind
Slipping
Towards insanity
Utters no cry
Held silent by a too empty room
That was never meant to be
I run, throw open
The door
Expecting more
memories cover sight
Then fade
Leaving empty reality
Too quiet to hear the questions
That aren't asked
Desperate, desperate
Screams in silence
Makes no dent
In the heavy quiet
Burdens a mind
Holding onto memories
With the volume turned down

44 Empty reality covers
The panicked mind
that fights for what it once
Thought it knew
Calling for who once stood
There, turns to the door
Raises a hand
With a kind smile
Calls echo through emptiness
Destroying the picture
A disappearing smile
Silence swore was never there
Whispers insecurity and insanity
Into the certain mind
Falls weak, turns, closes the door
An empty room, silent in silence,
Always empty.

My Heart Bleeds Red

My heart bleeds blue
The colour of the tears I cry for you
My heart bleeds blue
For all I've seen done to you
My heart bleeds blue
For all they put you through
My heart bleeds blue
Because you've stayed true
And it was never fair
The life you lived
The soul in you so rare
My heart bleeds blue
For all you hoped to do
I could never bear
The burden you carried
Would never have hoped to dare
My heart bleeds blue
Your heart always shone through
For promises never kept
And things I couldn't accept
For the empty words to you they said
My heart bleeds red.

46 Tell Me What I See

Tell me what I see
Through the mirror in my mind
Of my hopes and of my dreams
Running to extremes
If all that's in my way
Are the doubts of debts to pay
And all that I can see
Is right in front of me
And my ambition to buy
My way and my ride
Would I see I lied
Am I bonafide
With certs and stamps of approval
Saying I was here
Not whether there was fear
But if that's not what matters
With my rhythm get in gear
Through the mirror in my eyes
And the dreams that I see
Is the ever endless me
Always running extreme.

Like Ourselves

A bright side
For every gray moment
A silver lining
For every dark cloud
A candle flickering
In every shadowed window
Blank faces
That try but cannot see
Turn empty hearts
To feed on invisible hope
Like ghosts
Who float in lonely places
Where other ghosts
Seek them out
And we find them
Lingering in warm golden doorways
And peering in windows that show
Happy comforting moments
Like a television show/
Of Scrooge showering presents/
At the end of it all/
Everything they see with/
Empty eyes that rove and wander
For sight and a taste of what
They cannot see but feel there
Grasping at the edge of warmth
For a friendly corner
As all ghosts do
In lonely corners
On the edge of that dark cloud/
Looking at silver they wish they could have

48 They reach for what they cannot touch
Joined by ghosts
Similar in spirit
Whether sad or boisterous
Countenance shining
Tears or grin
Joined by ghosts
Like ourselves.

Man Made

Mechanical farce;
A pale comparison
Of the unaffected
Being
Constantly improving
On what is inherent
Until it is
An unrecognisable invention
Mass produced out of
All originality
Leaving steadily
Disappearing traces of
An inborn purity.

Ancient whispering oaks
Enfold my passing
While poplars chatter
And clusters of
Hemlock nod mute
Agreement in turn,
I wander dazed
Through this vivid
Wood. This place
Is my mystery,
Enigma of my soul
When nothing else
Makes sense I
Find myself here,
Accepting how little
I really know.
I am lost
In my own
Life I recognise
Nothing any more, a
Comfort then to
At least be
Lost in a
Place of such
Beauty.

50 Jerusalem: The Picture

An elliptical glass cage
Carries a miniature world
The hopes and doubts of millennia
Placed upon a frailty.
This cage is perfectly open
But few inside can escape
This frail, unyielding glass
And this world it goes on
Unchanging
A war of a different age
Its streets are the streets of yesterday
Tomorrow holds too little store.
So this world is full of
Uncertainty
And terror within and without
The burden its very foundation
The center of its rotation.
But loved for its weakest beauty
Who could not adore
So precious
This burden of feelings
he poorest weakest soul
Has the choice and choose
To carry this caged world
On his back.

Flowers and Clocks

Flowers bloom
In ticking clocks
Moments seen
In drops from a cloud
Your life
Held in Time's hand
Forget-Me-Nots
And daffodils that click
Every second
A Grandfather's face wreathed
By pretty blooms
A life's time in minutes watched
Mechanical hearts
Work miracles and chains around
Daily life
Binding with Ivy
Many hands
Tied up in the passing baby's breath
Held in never ending circles
Which fall
Racing to the bottom of the hourglass
Another way
Like a desert's seeds
As flowers bloom
In ticking clocks.

52 The Eye of the Beholder: An Ugly Thing

An ugly thing
That sits
Drawing attention from an otherwise
Beautiful room...

An eyesore
That takes up room
Who could love
Such an ugly thing...

And yet...
No dust gathers
Nothing covers the sight,
It shines in plain sight
Caressed by loving hands...
Such a beautiful thing,
Such a loved thing.

Time that
Weaves and drifts
Chains of ribbon
Around our lives
Invisibly binding us up
With lists of priority
Seen in a tumbling hourglass
That plans away
The days in our lives
Getting shorter
Spare minutes
In the form of
Single grains of sand
Slip away
As we are
Handcuffed to the
Hourglass' side
Yanking helplessly
Against Time's
Demanding bonds
A million reasons
In the mind's eye
Of Time tapping
Its wrist
As the voices
Of the day
Drop like
Acid rain
Into the
Wishes and dreams
Pulling tighter

54 The leash
Chafing our throats
Held
Unmercifully by Time
We fail to break free.

Defiance

Chaotic din
Declares my sin
With thunderous booming voice

So I fall
But hear my call
I'll not regret my choice.

Someone asked you for your help today
And you turned them away
It was easy enough for you to do
You have too much to lose.
You told me all the reasons you had to turn away
Though I didn't ask.
You didn't have
Enough money
Enough time
There was something wrong with their cause,
There was something wrong with them.
You didn't like their walk
Or the way they talked
Didn't like the way they dressed
The expression on their face
Or the one in their eyes.
They made you nervous,
Some indefinable thing about them.
You glared at me indignant
Though I didn't say anything
You couldn't connect with what they wanted,
That's all.
But-
You try to justify
What you won't give
And the cause of your nervousness
You just can't take.
You turn your face so you don't see,
Get angry with me
Though I didn't argue with them
Arguments you made.

56 Because I know the truth of it
I know you know it too
The thing about them you just
Couldn't like-
They were parts of you.

Shattered Shards

Shattered shards
Unbroken night
Multitudes of stars
Too damn bright
Lonely comet
Clamorous soul
Falling light
An unpayable toll.

Standing at
A window
As a spring wind blows
A hand
Pushing open
To better see
New buds rising
And all those green things...

A silhouette
Sitting by an open window
Summer heat
Broken by a stiff breeze
Outside people
Playing, laughing, living under a
Bright sun
Living under a bright sun...
 Writing by an open window
Looks up
A leaf drifting in
One leaf
In a season of falling
Of change
A colder wind blowing
New gray clouds cover once blue skies...

An open window
Pushed closed
By cold hands
Pull tighter
A robe for warmth

58 Not offered
By a season of ice
As a spring wind blows
A silhouette
Standing, pushes open
A window...

The Artist for Rebecca Joy Dando

Subtle brush lingers
Well settled in those familiar fingers
The strokes made on the page
As that Artist opens life's cage
To movements of Joy and flowing scenes;
Beyond all the complications and "what does it mean"'s
Quiet focus on what can be
Shaping the blank canvas to what Her inner eye sees
Each colour with deliberation picked
Unnoticing of the corner clock as it ticked
Every sweep of the brush making clearer
Visions of what makes something dearer
I simply watch in contemplation
Of the Artist at work, Her soul in isolation.

Is this it?
Have all our tomorrows
Faded to just one?
Our dawn
Has finally turned to dusk
And night falls quickly
In a world of only two.
Don't turn off the light
Just yet.
Don't turn away
Just yet.
In the dimming light
Kiss me once more
Like when our forever
Had only begun.
Pretend that the sun
Still hovers
On a golden horizon.
Pretend that the stars
Have not broken through
The cotton blue of our sky.
Ignore the moon
That silvers
The ruins of our love.
Don't step back
Just yet.
Don't fall asleep
Just yet.
In the hastening twilight
Hold me once more
Like when eternity

60 Encompassed us.
Even a condemned man
Gets a last meal.

I Miss the Moon

 I miss the moon;
A silly thing
I suppose.
For all that space is large,
For all seen gaseous stars,
For all room and saved mechanics,
Intellect, the brightest
From the dying planet
Rescued
All glory, all future
Light-speed ahead
And more planets still to discover;
I miss the trees before they faded
And the sky when it was still clear
I miss the animals when they were real-
This goes for the people too-
But most of all, a silly little thing-
I miss the moon.

If You Could

One wish
A chance to change
A single moment
Something strange
The hands of time
And a clock's ticking
A mirror's view
Of a life screaming and kicking
This very second
And a final choice
Could-be's and should-be's
Never given a voice
This is now
And what you would
A chance to be-
If you could.

A Pleasant Front

Basic paradoxical retorts simmer
Just under the façade of
Whimsy, a forced front
Sheltering Picasso pieces
Of altered perception-
Pivotal slips of memory
That provide an alibi for
Your failures and murmurings of unrest
A sense of anarchy
Built in childhood's chaos
Tangling like fairy knots

62 The twining seconds that
Make up what is "Now".

The Kind of Woman

You made sure I knew the kind of woman I was meant to be.
The kind of woman you would approve of.
The virtues I should have
And habits to reject.
You provided me a mold and told me how to grow.
For awhile it fit.
As a child I was malleable, formable.
But as I grew I stiffened.
My bones did not meld in your ways.
They were awkward and confined.
I couldn't breathe.
The mold cracked.
I clawed and stretched and pushed
Lungs burning and muscles aching
The mold was too small
When inside me was something so big.
I broke through.
I found the kind of woman
I wanted to be.
Not one you would approve of.
Not one that ticked off all your bullet points
Not one that spoke your words
And sang your songs.
I can breathe now
And I can't fit back into that mold.
I can't gain your approval now.
But I'm closer to gaining mine.
And that's okay.

Everything that is
Changes for new times
Moments for everything
As seasons turn cold
As grief fades
Everything changes
With new days
And possibilities for more
New chances
Filled with hope
Calls everything forward
Rather than standing still
Everything changes
Over time
Adaptation
And new feelings to replace old
Even anger must let go
Eventually
Everything changes
Winter to a colourful spring
Hope from despair
Learning new things
Learning to accept
Everything changes
Except a leopard's spots
They say it can't happen
But
Everything changes
I could change too.

Postscript

The poetry in this book was written from the time I was around twelve to when I was twenty-five. I wrote short stories as a child but when I was eleven, I had a teacher who wanted me to write a poem. Not a 'what am I? Spring' kind of poem or an 'I am' poem, just a poem. I quickly began writing more poems, enamored of the form of writing. Here was a way to express myself and the things that aren't always easy to say. During the 'lovely' teenage years it was a way for me to rant. At times it was a way to set down memories or express opinions. When my great grandpa died, I wrote a poem for him. When my grandpa died, I wrote another poem. I have written poems for my mother, for my friends, for me. I have written myself many poems. Sometimes they are not nice poems, but that is okay because everyone needs a way to get the poison out. I write to relax, I write because I enjoy it, and I write in the hopes that someone might find my poems interesting or pretty or comforting.

Readers may notice that some poems are in 'England English' and others are in 'American English'. This is because most of the poems were written when I was in America and I chose not to alter them.

To my family for their support and love no matter what.
To God for giving me a way to express myself so I don't blow up.

Index of First Lines

www.ingramcontent.com/pod-product-compliance
Lightning Source LLC
Chambersburg PA
CBHW060049050426
42448CB00011B/2370